Goethe

Eine Auswahl von Goethes bekanntesten lyrischen Werken. Ein neuer Weg, Goethe im Englischen zu lesen.

A Selection of Goethe's
best known lyrical Work.
An attempt
to find a new approach.

INHALTSVERZEICHNIS

CONTENTS

INHALTSVERZEICHNIS …

CONTENTS ...

Sturm und Drang Zeit

(1765 – 1790)

Sturm und Drang Period

(1765 – 1790)

An Luna

Schwester von dem ersten Licht,
Bild der Zärtlichkeit in Trauer,
Nebel schwimmt mit Silberschauer
Um dein reizendes Gesicht.
Deines leisen Fußes Lauf
Weckt aus tagverschlossnen Höhlen
Traurig abgeschiedne Seelen,
Mich, und nächt'ge Vögel auf.

Forschend übersieht dein Blick
Eine großgemessne Weite.
Hebe mich an deine Seite!
Gib der Schwärmerei dies Glück!
Und in wollustvoller Ruh
Sah' der weitverschlagne Ritter
Durch das gläserne Gegitter
Seines Mädchens Nächten zu.

To Luna

Sister of the light by day,
Image known for tenderness in grief!
Haze surrounds with silver fleece
Your adorably fair face;
Your silent foot along its path,
From caves, by daytime locked, arouses
Sadly hidden souls from their long drowses,
Me and birds nocturnal fast.

Exploring does your gaze then see
Areas of far extended vastness.
Let me sit with you abreast!
Grant my rapture such a bliss!
And with voluptuous ease
Did the widely strayed brave knight
Through the lattices by night
Watch his maid in her chemise.

An Luna …

Des Beschauens holdes Glück
Mildert solcher Ferne Qualen,
Und ich sammle deine Strahlen
Und ich schärfe meinen Blick;
Hell und heller wird es schon
Um die unverhüllten Glieder,
Und nun zieht sie mich hernieder,
Wie dich einst Endymion.

To Luna …

Lovely happiness while watching
Eases torments felt afar;
And I gather now your shafts,
And my vision I'm increasing.
Bright and brighter does it grow
Round the naked leg and arm,
And she pulls me down with charm,
Drawn like you by Endymion.

Wechsel

Auf Kieseln im Bache da lieg' ich, wie helle!
Verbreite die Arme der kommenden Welle,
Und buhlerisch drückt sie die sehnende Brust;
Dann führt sie der Leichtsinn im Strome danieder;
Es naht sich die zweite, sie streichelt mich wieder:
So fühl ich die Freuden der wechselnden Lust.

Und doch, und so traurig, verschleifst du vergebens
Die köstlichen Stunden des eilenden Lebens,
Weil dich das geliebteste Mädchen vergisst!
O ruf sie zurücke, die vorigen Zeiten!
Es küsst sich so süße die Lippe der Zweiten,
Als kaum sich die Lippe der Ersten geküsst.

Change

On pebbles I lie there, how smart!
Spread out the arms the next wave toward,
It nestles against the bosom aquiver,
Its levity leads it downwards the river,
There comes the second, it strokes me again,
So I enjoy the passion that offers a change.

Yet and so sadly in vain you waste
The delicious times in life that do race,
Because the darling maid you does leave!
Oh, call them back the times bygone,
The lips of the second, they tasted so strong,
The lips of the first could hardly compete.

An Die Entfernte

So hab' ich wirklich dich verloren,
Bist du, o Schöne, mir entflohn?
Noch klingt in den gewohnten Ohren
Ein jedes Wort, ein jeder Ton.

So wie des Wandrers Blick am Morgen
Vergebens in die Lüfte dringt,
Wenn, in dem blauen Raum verborgen,
Hoch über ihm die Lerche singt;

So dringet ängstlich hin und wieder
Durch Feld und Busch und Wald mein Blick;
Dich rufen alle meine Lieder;
O komm, Geliebte, mir zurück!

To The Distant

So have you truly gone away?
Did you, oh beauty, flee from me?
Still do I hear you »love you« say
And all the words that you did speak.

So like the rambler's eyes in vain
Does search the wide sky in the morning,
When hidden in the blue of space,
Above him does the lark there sing.

Thus search my eyes most timidly
Field, bush and forest longingly.
As all my songs do call for thee,
Oh come, my darling, back to me!

Mailied

Wie herrlich leuchtet
Mir die Natur!
Wie glänzt die Sonne!
Wie lacht die Flur!

Es dringen Blüten
Aus jedem Zweig
Und tausend Stimmen
Aus dem Gesträuch.

Und Freud' und Wonne
Aus jeder Brust.
O Erd', o Sonne!
O Glück, o Lust!

May Song

How lovely shines
The world I see!
How beams the sun!
How laughs the field!

Blossoms grow
On every branch
And thousand sounds
From shrubs do chant.

And joy and fun
Fill every breast
Oh earth, oh sun!
Oh glee, oh zest!

Mailied …

O Lieb', o Liebe!
So golden schön,
Wie Morgenwolken
Auf jenen Höhn!

Du segnest herrlich
Das frische Feld,
Im Blütendampfe
Die volle Welt.

O Mädchen, o Mädchen,
Wie lieb ich dich!
Wie blinkt dein Auge!
Wie liebst du mich!

May Song …

Oh dear, oh love!
So gold and fair!
Like morning clouds
On heights up there!

You bless so pleasant
The waking soil,
In flowers` scent
The world overall.

Oh beauty, oh beauty,
How I do love thee!
How charm your eyes!
How you do love me!

Mailied …

So liebt die Lerche
Gesang und Luft,
Und Morgenblumen
Den Himmelsduft,

Wie ich dich liebe
Mit warmen Blut,
Die du mir Jugend
Und Freud' und Mut

Zu neuen Liedern
Und Tänzen gibst.
Sei ewig glücklich,
Wie du mich liebst!

May Song …

Thus loves the lark
Breezes and chant,
And early flowers,
The sky`s soft balm.

How I do love you
With blood`s full heat,
My youth you boost
And joy and grit

For great new songs
And dances above.
Be happy a life long,
With me your great love.!

Heidenröslein

Sah ein Knab' ein Röslein stehn,
Röslein auf der Heiden,
War so jung und morgenschön,
Lief er schnell, es nah zu sehn,
Sah's mit vielen Freuden.
Röslein, Röslein, Röslein rot,
Röslein auf der Heiden.

Knabe sprach: »Ich breche dich,
Röslein auf der Heiden!«
Röslein sprach: »Ich steche dich,
Dass du ewig denkst an mich,
Und ich will's nicht leiden.«
Röslein, Röslein, Röslein rot,
Röslein auf der Heiden.

Rose On The Heath

Saw a lad a rose fine bloom,
Rose that grows there on the heath,
Was so young and beautiful,
Ran to see as close he could,
Saw it with a lot of glee.
Rose so dear and rose so red,
Rose that grows there on the heath.

Lad then said: »I`ll pluck you now,
Rose that grows there on the heath!«
Rose yet said: »I`ll prick then thou,
That you`ll always think of me,
And I will not suffer it.«
Rose so dear and rose so red,
Rose that grows there on the heath.

Heidenröslein …

Und der wilde Knabe brach
's Röslein auf der Heiden;
Röslein wehrte sich und stach,
Half ihm doch kein Weh und Ach,
Musst' es eben leiden.
Röslein, Röslein, Röslein rot,
Röslein auf der Heiden.

Rose On The Heath …

And the savage lad did pluck
Rose that grows there on the heath;
Rose then pricked and fiercely struck,
Didn`t help him cry alack,
Had to simply suffer deep.
Rose so dear and rose so red,
Rose that grows there on the heath.

Ach, Wie Sehn Ich Mich Nach Dir

Ach, wie sehn' ich mich nach dir,
Kleiner Engel! Nur im Traum,
Nur im Traum erscheine mir!
Ob ich da gleich viel erleide,
Bang um dich mit Geistern streite,
Und erwachend atme kaum.
Ach, wie sehn' ich mich nach dir,
Ach, wie teuer bist du mir
Selbst in einem schweren Traum.

Oh, How Do I Long For You

Oh, how do I long for you,
Little angel! When I dream
Shall your vision turn out true!
Whether I must suffer trouble,
Worrying with spirits struggle,
Waking do I hardly breathe.
Oh, how do I long for thee,
Oh, how dear are you to me,
Eke when harm upsets my dream.

Willkommen Und Abschied

Es schlug mein Herz. Geschwind zu Pferde!
Und fort, wild wie ein Held zur Schlacht.
Der Abend wiegte schon die Erde,
Und an den Bergen hing die Nacht.
Schon stund im Nebelkleid die Eiche
Wie ein getürmter Riese da,
Wo Finsternis aus dem Gesträuche
Mit hundert schwarzen Augen sah.

Der Mond von einem Wolkenhügel
Sah schläfrig aus dem Duft hervor,
Die Winde schwangen leise Flügel,
Umsausten schauerlich mein Ohr.
Die Nacht schuf tausend Ungeheuer,
Doch tausendfacher war mein Mut,
Mein Geist war ein verzehrend Feuer,
Mein ganzes Herz zerfloss in Glut.

Welcome And Farewell

My heart throbbed fast. Quick, mount the horse!
Off, like a hero seeking the fight.
The eve already had started its course,
And at the mountains waved the night.
Clad in a veil of mist stood there the oak,
A towering giant like,
Where darkness from the forest`s cloak
Looked with a hundred blackish eyes.

The moon there from a hill of cloud
Looked drowsily through misty haze,
The wings of the winds now flapped about,
Whirled round my ear, a horrible chase.
The night bore monsters thousandfold,
Yet still more thousandfold my courage was.
My mind was driven by a force untold,
And all my heart with heat did glow.

Willkommen Und Abschied ...

Ich sah dich, und die milde Freude
Floss aus dem süßen Blick auf mich.
Ganz war mein Herz an deiner Seite,
Und jeder Atemzug für dich.
Ein rosenfarbnes Frühlingswetter
Lag auf dem lieblichen Gesicht
Und Zärtlichkeit für mich, ihr Götter,
Ich hofft' es, ich verdient' es nicht.

Der Abschied, wie bedrängt, wie trübe!
Aus deinen Blicken sprach dein Herz.
In deinen Küssen welche Liebe,
O welche Wonne, welcher Schmerz!
Du gingst, ich stund und sah zur Erden
Und sah dir nach mit nassem Blick.
Und doch, welch Glück, geliebt zu werden,
Und lieben, Götter, welch ein Glück!

Welcome And Farewell …

I saw you, and the gentle pleasure
Poured from your sweet eyes onto me.
For all my heart you were a treasure,
And breathing did I but for thee.
Rose-coloured like a springtime weather,
That was the look on your beloved face!
And tendresse just for me, what could be better,
Though undeserved, my hope yet did it raise.

The farewell, how so hurting, and how bleak!
Your eyes told me your heart then spoke.
Great love your kisses promised me,
Oh such a bliss, such woe!
You left, I stayed and looked at an abyss,
And followed then your steps with tear-stained eyes.
Yet to be loved means such a bliss,
To love, oh gods, how dear a prize!

Neue Liebe, Neues Leben

Herz, mein Herz, was soll das geben?
Was bedränget dich so sehr?
Welch ein fremdes, neues Leben!
Ich erkenne dich nicht mehr.
Weg ist alles, was du liebtest,
Weg, warum du dich betrübtest,
Weg dein Fleiß und deine Ruh –
Ach, wie kamst du nur dazu?

Fesselt dich die Jugendblüte,
Diese liebliche Gestalt,
Dieser Blick voll Treu' und Güte
Mit unendlicher Gewalt?
Will ich rasch mich ihr entziehen,
Mich ermannen, ihr entfliehen,
Führet mich im Augenblick
Ach, mein Weg zu ihr zurück.

New Love, New Life

Heart, my heart, what is your plan?
What may harass you so much?
What a life so new and foreign!
I haven`t known you yet as such.
Gone all what you once had loved,
Gone, why you had felt oft lost,
Gone your effort and your calm –
Oh, what is it you have done?

Does the flush of youth enthral you,
That sweet shape that looks so light,
That look full of faith and truth
With a never-ending might?
If I quickly run from her,
Find the courage now and leave her,
Yet my way leads at this moment,
Back, alas, to her, such a bad omen.

Neue Liebe, Neues Leben ...

Und an diesem Zauberfädchen,
Das sich nicht zerreißen lässt,
Hält das liebe lose Mädchen,
Mich so wider Willen fest.
Muss in ihrem Zauberkreise
Leben nun auf ihre Weise.
Die Verändrung, ach, wie groß!
Liebe, Liebe, lass mich los!

New Love, New Life …

Shackled at that magic thread,
That cannot easily be torn,
Does that good and wanton maid
Keep unwillingly me bound,
Must I drawn by her great magic
Live as she does, which is tragic.
Oh, how great is there the change!
Love dear love give me some range!

Der König In Thule

Es war ein König in Thule
Gar treu bis an das Grab,
Dem sterbend seine Buhle
Einen goldnen Becher gab.

Es ging ihm nichts darüber,
Er leert' ihn jeden Schmaus;
Die Augen gingen ihm über,
Sooft er trank daraus.

Und als er kam zu sterben,
Zählt' er seine Städt' im Reich,
Gönnt' alles seinem Erben,
Den Becher nicht zugleich.

The King In Thule

In Thule once there was a king,
So faithful unto his grave,
To whom his love when dying
A golden chalice gave.

He was about it full of glee,
He emptied it when he did dine;
His eyes then sparkled happily,
When from it he drank wine.

When time then came to die,
He counted all his towns,
Gave all his sons he had laid by,
The chalice yet remained his own.

Der König In Thule …

Er saß beim Königsmahle,
Die Ritter um ihn her,
Auf hohem Vätersaale,
Dort auf dem Schloss am Meer.

Dort stand der alte Zecher,
Trank letzte Lebensglut,
Und warf den heil'gen Becher
Hinunter in die Flut.

Er sah ihn stürzen, trinken
Und sinken tief ins Meer.
Die Augen täten ihm sinken;
Trank nie einen Tropfen mehr.

The King in Thule ...

For feasting with him did he call,
His knights to come and eat,
Sat with them in his father's hall,
There in the castle by the sea.

There stood the aged reveller,
Drank still a gulp his eyes aglow,
Threw then the sacred beaker
Into the sea below.

He saw it fall and filling,
Sink deep onto the ocean floor,
His eyes closed then unwilling;
And drink did he no more.

Wandrers Nachtlied I

Der du von dem Himmel bist,
Alles Leid und Schmerzen stillest,
Den, der doppelt elend ist,
Doppelt mit Erquickung füllest,
Ach, ich bin des Treibens müde,
Was soll all der Schmerz und Lust?
Süßer Friede,
Komm, ach komm in meine Brust!

Rambler`s Nightsong I

You who comes from heaven yet,
All the woes and pains can still,
Him who feels so doubly bad,
Twofold with relief will fill,
All the striving tires me!
So what, anguish and great lust?
Come sweet peace,
Come, calm my troubled breast!

Rastlose Liebe

Dem Schnee, dem Regen,
Dem Wind entgegen,
Im Dampf der Klüfte,
Durch Nebeldüfte,
Immer zu! Immer zu!
Ohne Rast und Ruh!

Lieber durch Leiden
Möcht' ich mich schlagen,
Als so viel Freuden
Des Lebens ertragen.
Alle das Neigen
Von Herzen zu Herzen,
Ach, wie so eigen
Schaffet das Schmerzen!

Wie soll ich fliehen?
Wälderwärts ziehen?
Alles vergebens!
Krone des Lebens,
Glück ohne Ruh,
Liebe bist Du!

Restless Love

The wind in the face,
The snow and the rain,
In the ravine`s steam,
Through fog`s perfume,
On you go!
No rest you know!

Would rather suffer
The hardship of woe,
Than all the pleasure
In life to bear though.
All the close leaning
From heart toward heart
Oh, how alarming
It does really smart!

How shall I fly?
In forests hide?
All is for nothing!
Life's efforts crowning,
Resting won`t do,
Love´s sure you!

Der Fischer

Das Wasser rauscht', das Wasser schwoll,
Ein Fischer saß daran,
Sah nach dem Angel ruhevoll,
Kühl bis ans Herz hinan.
Und wie er sitzt, und wie er lauscht,
Teilt sich die Flut empor;
Aus dem bewegten Wasser rauscht
Ein feuchtes Weib hervor.

The Fisherman

A fisher hears the water roar,
He eyes his rod at ease and calm,
When sitting placidly ashore,
His heartbeat cool, not sensing harm.
As sitting there and listening,
The waves then part and open wide;
Out of the water glistening,
A soaky woman comes into sight.

Der Fischer …

Sie sang zu ihm, sie sprach zu ihm:
»Was lockst du meine Brut
Mit Menschenwitz und Menschenlist
Hinauf in Todesglut?
Ach wüsstest du, wie's Fischlein ist
So wohlig auf dem Grund,
Du stiegst herunter, wie du bist,
Und würdest erst gesund.

Labt sich die liebe Sonne nicht,
Der Mond sich nicht im Meer?
Kehrt wellenatmend ihr Gesicht
Nicht doppelt schöner her?
Lockt dich der tiefe Himmel nicht,
Das feuchtverklärte Blau?
Lockt dich dein eigen Angesicht
Nicht her in ew'gen Tau?«

The Fisherman …

She sang to him and spoke to him:
»Why do you lure my brood
With human wit and human whim
Up to their death as human food?
Oh, if you knew how fishes feel
So blissful in the water`s deep,
You would jump down not paying heed
Where then you wouldn`t be in need.

Does not the sun so kind to us
Feast on the sea and also moon?
Does not her face upon the waves
Gain such twice lovelier a look?
Does sky`s large depth not mean a lure
The soaky splender of the blue?
Does not tempt you the face of yours
To dive up from eternal dew?«

Der Fischer …

Das Wasser rauscht', das Wasser schwoll,
Netzt' ihm den nackten Fuß;
Sein Herz wuchs ihm so sehnsuchtsvoll,
Wie bei der Liebsten Gruß.
Sie sprach zu ihm, sie sang zu ihm;
Da war's um ihn geschehn:
Halb zog sie ihn, halb sank er hin,
Und ward nicht mehr gesehn.

The Fisherman …

The water rushes, the water rises,
It wets his naked foot,
His heart grows heavy with desire,
Just as his darling`s greeting could.
She spoke to him he heard her sing,
That made him lose his mind,
Half did she pull, half did he sink,
And no one could again him find.

Der Erlkönig

Wer reitet so spät durch Nacht und Wind?
Es ist der Vater mit seinem Kind;
Er hat den Knaben wohl in dem Arm,
Er fasst ihn sicher, er hält ihn warm. –

The Erlking

Who rides that late by storm and night?
It is the father with his child;
He holds the lad well in his arm,
He grips him tight, he keeps him warm.

Der Erlkönig …

Mein Sohn, was birgst du so bang dein Gesicht? –
Siehst, Vater, du den Erlkönig nicht?
Den Erlenkönig mit Kron' und Schweif? –
Mein Sohn, es ist ein Nebelstreif. –

»Du liebes Kind, komm, geh mit mir!
Gar schöne Spiele spiel' ich mit dir;
Manch' bunte Blumen sind an dem Strand;
Meine Mutter hat manch' gülden Gewand.«

Mein Vater, mein Vater, und hörest du nicht,
Was Erlenkönig mir leise verspricht? –
Sei ruhig, bleibe ruhig, mein Kind!
In dürren Blättern säuselt der Wind. –

The Erlking …

»My son, why do you hide your face in fear?«
»Can`t you, my father, see Erlking so near?
The Erlking there with crown and tail?«
»My son, it`s a wisp of fog without fail.«

»My dear child come and go with me!
Will wonderfully play with thee,
Some lovely flowers fringe the shore,
My mother owns nice robes galore.«

»My father, my father and don`t you hear,
How Erlking`s promises sound so dear?«
»Stay quiet, stay quiet, my dearest child;
The whispering wind lets the dry leaves sigh.«

Der Erlkönig …

»Willst, feiner Knabe, du mit mir gehn?
Meine Töchter sollen dich warten schön;
Meine Töchter führen den nächtlichen Reihn
Und wiegen und tanzen und singen dich ein.«

Mein Vater, mein Vater, und siehst du nicht dort
Erlkönigs Töchter am düstern Ort? –
Mein Sohn, mein Sohn, ich seh' es genau;
Es scheinen die alten Weiden so grau. –

»Ich liebe dich, mich reizt deine schöne Gestalt;
Und bist du nicht willig, so brauch' ich Gewalt.« –
Mein Vater, mein Vater, jetzt fasst er mich an!
Erlkönig hat mir ein Leids getan! –

The Erlking …

»You fancy, fine boy, to come with me?
My daughters so lovely shall care for thee;
My daughters keep leading the nightly round,
They`ll rock you safe with their dance and song.«

»My father, my father don`t you see in their masquerade
Erlking`s daughters in the dark there wait?«
»My son, my son, I see that, I`ll say!
Those are just willows old and grey.«

»Your gracious shape has spurred my desire;
And if you`re unwilling, you`ll be in the mire.«
»My father, my father he touches me, see!
Erlking has done now harm to me.«

Der Erlkönig …

Dem Vater grauset's, er reitet geschwind,
Er hält in Armen das ächzende Kind,
Erreicht den Hof mit Mühe und Not;
In seinen Armen das Kind war tot.

The Erlking …

The father grows anxious, he hastens the ride,
He holds in his arms the groaning child,
He reaches the farm driven by dread;
But the child in his arms already is dead.

Ein Gleiches
Wandrers Nachtlied II

Über allen Gipfeln
Ist Ruh',
In allen Wipfeln
Spürest Du
Kaum einen Hauch;
Die Vögelein schweigen im Walde.
Warte nur, balde
Ruhest du auch.

Alike

Rambler's Nightsong II

Over all the peaks
Is peace,
In all the trees
You perceive
Scarce a move;
The wood`s birds rest,
And you`d wait best,
You`ll sleep soon, too.

Freudvoll Und Leidvoll

Freudvoll
Und leidvoll,
Gedankenvoll sein,
Langen
Und bangen
In schwebender Pein,
Himmelhoch jauchzend,
Zum Tode betrübt;
Glücklich allein
Ist die Seele, die liebt.

Joyful And Sorrowful

Joyful
And sorrowful.
Thoughtful to be
Wishing
And Worrying
In doubtful agony,
Rejoycing sky-high,
Deathly downcast,
Blissful in life
Is the soul that loves.

An Den Mond

Füllest wieder Busch und Tal
Still mit Nebelglanz,
Lösest endlich auch einmal
Meine Seele ganz;

Breitest über mein Gefild
Lindernd deinen Blick,
Wie des Freundes Auge mild
Über mein Geschick.

Jeden Nachklang fühlt mein Herz
Froh- und trüber Zeit,
Wandle zwischen Freud' und Schmerz
In der Einsamkeit.

To The Moon

Bush and dale you fill again
Still with hazy shine,
Thus you loosen on this day
All the soul of mine;

And you cast across my clime
Soothingly your light,
Like a friend`s so lenient eye,
You dwell on the feel of mine.

Every echo feels my heart
Of times merry or yet rude,
Walk twixt happiness and smart
In the quiet solitude.

An Den Mond …

Fließe, fließe, lieber Fluss!
Nimmer werd' ich froh,
So verrauschte Scherz und Kuss,
Und die Treue so.

Ich besaß es doch einmal,
Was so köstlich ist!
Dass man doch zu seiner Qual
Nimmer es vergisst!

Rausche, Fluss, das Tal entlang,
Ohne Rast und Ruh,
Rausche, flüstre meinem Sang
Melodien zu,

To The Moon …

Flow you river do not stay!
Never will I ever cheer,
Fun and kisses passed away,
And so did all loyalty.

I had found it yet one day,
What but means great pleasure!
Yet becomes such aching pain
You will not forget for ever!

Rush, dear river, down the vale,
Without rest or calm,
Rush and whisper on your way
Lovely tunes backing my chant.

An Den Mond …

Wenn du in der Winternacht
Wütend überschwillst,
Oder um die Frühlingspracht
Junger Knospen quillst.

Selig, wer sich vor der Welt
Ohne Hass verschließt,
Einen Freund am Busen hält
Und mit dem genießt,

Was, von Menschen nicht gewusst
Oder nicht bedacht,
Durch das Labyrinth der Brust
Wandelt in der Nacht.

To The Moon …

When you in the winter`s night
With much fury overspill,
Or around spring`s glorious sight
Of young buds you rill.

Blissful who on this rude world
Turns his back but without hate,
Has a friend who stirs his heart,
And with whom he shares his fate.

What, unknown to every human
Or just totally ignored,
Through the bosom`s confusion
Is walking in the dark.

Die Zeit der Weimarer Klassik

(1790 – 1832)

The period of Weimar Classicism

(1790 – 1832)

Nur Wer Die Sehnsucht Kennt

Nur wer die Sehnsucht kennt,
Weiß, was ich leide!
Allein und abgetrennt
Von aller Freude,
Seh' ich ans Firmament
Nach jener Seite.

Ach! der mich liebt und kennt,
Ist in der Weite.
Es schwindelt mir, es brennt
Mein Eingeweide.
Nur wer die Sehnsucht kennt,
Weiß, was ich leide!

Just Who Does Longing feel

Just who does longing feel
Will know how much I suffer!
Deserted, lost and be
Now robbed of any pleasure,
At our firmament I see
Towards that side over there.

He who knows and loves me,
Has now gone far away.
I`m dizzy and I feel
My bowles weigh much rougher.
Just who does longing feel,
Will know how much I suffer!

Der Schatzgräber

Arm am Beutel, krank am Herzen,
Schleppt' ich meine langen Tage.
Armut ist die größte Plage,
Reichtum ist das höchste Gut!
Und zu enden meine Schmerzen,
Ging ich, einen Schatz zu graben.
»Meine Seele sollst du haben!«
Schrieb ich hin mit eignem Blut.

Und so zog ich Kreis' um Kreise,
Stellte wunderbare Flammen,
Kraut und Knochenwerk zusammen:
Die Beschwörung war vollbracht.
Und auf die gelernte Weise
Grub ich nach dem alten Schatze
Auf dem angezeigten Platze.
Schwarz und stürmisch war die Nacht.

The Treasure Hunter

With empty pockets and poor health,
Did I spend my boring days.
Poverty is a great malaise,
The highest value sure is wealth!
So to end my steady pain,
Did I go to seek a treasure.
»In my soul you shall now reign!«
Did I write with blood on paper.

So I drew quite many a ring,
Used some magic fire that would bring ,
Herbs and bone combine to one;
Now the magic art was done.
Taking to my learned trade
Did I dig for hoard once laid
At the place announced to me:
The night was dark, raged violently.

Der Schatzgräber ...

Und ich sah ein Licht von weiten,
Und es kam gleich einem Sterne
Hinten aus der fernsten Ferne,
Eben als es zwölfe schlug.
Und da galt kein Vorbereiten.
Heller ward's mit einem Male
Von dem Glanz der vollen Schale,
Die ein schöner Knabe trug.

Holde Augen sah ich blinken
Unter dichtem Blumenkranze;
In des Trankes Himmelsglanze
Trat er in den Kreis herein.
Und er hieß mich freundlich trinken;
Und ich dacht': es kann der Knabe
Mit der schönen lichten Gabe
Wahrlich nicht der Böse sein.

The Treasure Hunter …

And I saw a light from far,
That came like a shining star
From a distance far way back,
Twelve o`clock the hour struck.
Now there`s no time to tarry.
Brighter grew the night now steady
By the full bowl`s sudden light,
Carried by a handsome child.

Lovely eyes I saw there gleam
From beneath a floral wreath;
In the brilliance of the drink
Did he step into the ring.
Then he bid me have a try;
And I thought that friendly child
With the shining offering
Cannot be the evil fiend.

Der Schatzgräber ...

»Trinke Mut des reinen Lebens!
Dann verstehst du die Belehrung,
Kommst mit ängstlicher Beschwörung
Nicht zurück an diesen Ort.
Grabe hier nicht mehr vergebens!
Tages Arbeit, abends Gäste!
Saure Wochen, frohe Feste!
Sei dein künftig Zauberwort.«

The Treasure Hunter …

»Drink the spirit of pure life!
That`s a lecture to comply,
Timid magic thwarts a way
To come back here for a stay.
Digging here will be in vain.
Work by day! And guests by night
Merry feasting! Weeks just plain!
Be your magic word all right.«

Der Zauberlehrling

Hat der alte Hexenmeister
Sich doch einmal wegbegeben!
Und nun sollen seine Geister
Auch nach meinem Willen leben.
Seine Wort' und Werke
Merkt' ich und den Brauch,
Und mit Geistesstärke
Tu' ich Wunder auch.

The Sorcerer's Apprentice

Has the aged sorcerer
Gone at last away one time!
Now his spirits as my helpers
Shall act on the word of mine.
All the old man`s words he spoke
Did I learn for later use,
All my strength will I invoke
And thus wonders I will do.

Der Zauberlehrling …

Walle! walle!
Manche Strecke,
Dass zum Zwecke
Wasser fließe,
Und mit reichem, vollem Schwalle
Zu dem Bade sich ergieße!

Und nun komm, du alter Besen!
Nimm die schlechten Lumpenhüllen!
Bist schon lange Knecht gewesen;
Nun erfülle meinen Willen!
Auf zwei Beinen stehe,
Oben sei ein Kopf,
Eile nun und gehe
Mit dem Wassertopf!

The Sorcerer's Apprentice ...

Bubble! Bubble!
Quite a stretch,
So that thus
Water rushes,
And in large a flush
Down into the basin gushes!

You old broomstick come along!
Take the rag the useless one!
As a menial you've served long;
Now on my command you run!
On two legs you walk,
Up there be your head,
Hurry now, don`t talk!
Carry water don`t forget!

Der Zauberlehrling …

Walle! walle!
Manche Strecke,
Dass zum Zwecke
Wasser fließe,
Und mit reichem, vollem Schwalle
Zu dem Bade sich ergieße!

Seht, er läuft zum Ufer nieder;
Wahrlich! ist schon an dem Flusse,
Und mit Blitzesschnelle wieder
Ist er hier mit raschem Gusse.
Schon zum zweiten Male!
Wie das Becken schwillt!
Wie sich jede Schale
Voll mit Wasser füllt!

The Sorcerer's Apprentice ...

Bubble! Bubble!
Quite a stretch.
So that thus,
Water rushes
And in large a flush
Down into the basin gushes!

Look, he runs yet to the bank,
Truly, has just reached the river,
Quick as lightning comes again
With the bucket to deliver
And so for the second time!
How the basin fills with water!
And with every bowl will climb,
Yet though filled, he doesn`t falter.

Der Zauberlehrling ...

Stehe! stehe!
Denn wir haben
Deiner Gaben
Vollgemessen! –
Ach, ich merk' es! Wehe! wehe!
Hab' ich doch das Wort vergessen!

Ach, das Wort, worauf am Ende
Er das wird, was er gewesen.
Ach, er läuft und bringt behende!
Wärst du doch der alte Besen!
Immer neue Güsse
Bringt er schnell herein,
Ach! und hundert Flüsse
Stürzen auf mich ein.

The Sorcerer's Apprentice …

Stop it! Stop it!
For your art
Helped me start,
Be deterred!
Oh, I see! And woe to me!
I forgot the magic word!

Yes, the word to turn him back
Into what he was before.
Still he runs and need not slack!
Wished you served me never more!
Buckets filled up to the brim
Does he quickly carry hither,
Cannot help myself but swim,
All around me flows a river.

Der Zauberlehrling …

Nein, nicht länger
Kann ich's lassen;
Will ihn fassen.
Das ist Tücke!
Ach! nun wird mir immer bänger!
Welche Miene! welche Blicke!

O, du Ausgeburt der Hölle!
Soll das ganze Haus ersaufen?
Seh' ich über jede Schwelle
Doch schon Wasserströme laufen.
Ein verruchter Besen,
Der nicht hören will!
Stock, der du gewesen,
Steh doch wieder still!

The Sorcerer's Apprentice …

Not any longer
Can I watch.
Him I'll catch.
Such a guile!
Now I feel my scare grow stronger!
Mien and look are yet so vile!

Oh, you fiendish creature!
Is your wish to drown the house?
Everywhere I see just water
Torrents threat the house to douse.
Wicked broomstick,
Listen, won`t you!
Be your doom it,
Be again a lifeless tool!

Der Zauberlehrling ...

Willst's am Ende
Gar nicht lassen?
Will dich fassen,
Will dich halten,
Und das alte Holz behende
Mit dem scharfen Beile spalten.

Seht, da kommt er schleppend wieder!
Wie ich mich nur auf dich werfe,
Gleich, o Kobold, liegst du nieder;
Krachend trifft die glatte Schärfe!
Wahrlich, brav getroffen!
Seht, er ist entzwei!
Und nun kann ich hoffen,
Und ich atme frei!

The Sorcerer's Apprentice …

Don`t you want to
Stop at all?
Want your downfall,
Wish to seize you
And to split the stick in two,
Which a sharp axe fast will do.

There you come back water dragging!
How I lunge at you with might,
Soon, oh monster, are you gasping,
Now the axe`s sheath does strike!
Yes, it is a deadly hit!
Look, the fiend is truly split!
And my hope is now fulfilled,
I breathe freely, he is killed.

Der Zauberlehrling …

Wehe! wehe!
Beide Teile
Stehn in Eile
Schon als Knechte
Völlig fertig in die Höhe!
Helft mir, ach! ihr hohen Mächte!

Und sie laufen! Nass und nässer
Wird's im Saal und auf den Stufen.
Welch entsetzliches Gewässer!
Herr und Meister! hör' mich rufen! –
Ach, da kommt der Meister!
Herr, die Not ist groß!
Die ich rief, die Geister,
Werd' ich nun nicht los.

The Sorcerer's Apprentice …

Poor me! poor me!
The two parts
Stand at once
Upright fully
Ready for their task!
Help me, higher powers, fast!

There they run! Wet and wetter
Hall and steps already turn.
How the dreadful currents churn!
Lord and master help me, better!
Oh, I see my master come!
Lord, the mess I`m in is great!
Woe, the spirits I did summon,
They are sadly still awake.

Der Zauberlehrling ...

»In die Ecke,
Besen! Besen!
Seid's gewesen.
Denn als Geister
Ruft euch nur, zu seinem Zwecke,
Erst hervor der alte Meister.«

The Sorcerer's Apprentice …

»In the corner,
Broomstick! Broomstick!
Done now is your evil trick!
For as spirits
Are you summoned by your master
Only when he sees it fit.«

Frühzeitiger Frühling

Tage der Wonne,
Kommt ihr so bald?
Schenkt mir die Sonne,
Hügel und Wald?

Reichlicher fließen
Bächlein zumal.
Sind es die Wiesen,
Ist es das Tal?

Blauliche Frische!
Himmel und Höh'!
Goldene Fische
Wimmeln im See.

Early Spring

Days of delight,
Will you come still?
Will me sun`s light
Gift wood and hill?

More forcefully flow
Brooklets so well.
Is it the meadow?
Is it the dell?

Refreshing breeze!
Blue sky and hill!
Golden fish
Do the lake fill.

Frühzeitiger Frühling …

Buntes Gefieder
Rauschet im Hain;
Himmlische Lieder
Schallen darein.

Unter des Grünen
Blühender Kraft
Naschen die Bienen
Summend am Saft.

Leise Bewegung
Bebt in der Luft,
Reizende Regung,
Schläfernder Duft.

Early Spring …

Colourful plumes
Rush in the grove,
Heavenly tunes
Sound from above.

Under the green`s
Blooming vigour,
Guzzle the bees,
Buzzing, the liquor

Silent movement
Throbs in the air,
Lovely excitement,
Drowsy smell there.

Frühzeitiger Frühling …

Mächtiger rühret
Bald sich ein Hauch,
Doch er verlieret
Gleich sich im Strauch.

Aber zum Busen
Kehrt er zurück.
Helfet, ihr Musen,
Tragen das Glück!

Saget, seit gestern
Wie mir geschah?
Liebliche Schwestern,
Liebchen ist da!

Early Spring …

With force there stirs
A soft waft soon,
Yet does disperse
At once in the bloom.

But to the bosom
Does it come back.
Help me you Muses
Bliss not to lack!

Say, since a day ago,
How did I fare?
Dearest sisters, lo,
Darling is there!

Osterspaziergang

Vom Eise befreit sind Strom und Bäche
Durch des Frühlings holden, belebenden Blick;
Im Tale grünet Hoffnungsglück;
Der alte Winter, in seiner Schwäche,
Zog sich in rauhe Berge zurück.
Von dorther sendet er, fliehend, nur
Ohnmächtige Schauer körnigen Eises
In Streifen über die grünende Flur;
Aber die Sonne duldet kein Weißes,
Überall regt sich Bildung und Streben,
Alles will sie mit Farben beleben;
Doch an Blumen fehlt's im Revier,
Sie nimmt geputzte Menschen dafür.

Easter Walk

Freed from ice are rivers and brook
Thanks to spring`s enlivening breeze,
The valley`s green`s a promising look.
Old Winter's force grows slowly weak,
Lets him withdraw to harsher heights,
From where he sends on his retreat
Faint downpours mixed with grainy ice
Streaking the fields´ fast-growing green.
The sun does not allow of white,
Forming and striving do everywhere stir,
Colours shall turn all the greyness bright;
Flowers yet are still missing there,
It takes well-groomed men instead.

Osterspaziergang ...

Kehre dich um, von diesen Höhen
Nach der Stadt zurückzusehen.
Aus dem hohlen, finstern Tor
Dringt ein buntes Gewimmel hervor.
Jeder sonnt sich heute so gern.
Sie feiern die Auferstehung des Herrn,
Denn sie sind selber auferstanden,
Aus niedriger Häuser dumpfen Gemächern,
Aus Handwerks- und Gewerbesbanden,
Aus dem Druck von Giebeln und Dächern,
Aus der Straßen quetschender Enge,
Aus der Kirchen ehrwürdiger Nacht
Sind sie alle ans Licht gebracht.

Easter Walk …

Turn around, from this green region,
Look towards the town this season.
Out of the narrow, darkish gate
A colourful throng comes into sight.
All enjoying a sunbath today
Celebrating the resurrection of Jesus Christ,
For they themselves have come alive:
Left their homes and their dull places,
Workshops and free enterprise,
Escaped the squeeze of roofs and gables,
The crushing closeness of the street,
The churches` sacred night with speed,
And are at last now free to breathe.

Osterspaziergang …

Sieh nur, sieh! wie behend sich die Menge
Durch die Gärten und Felder zerschlägt,
Wie der Fluss in Breit' und Länge
So manchen lustigen Nachen bewegt,
Und bis zum Sinken überladen
Entfernt sich dieser letzte Kahn.
Selbst von des Berges fernen Pfaden
Blinken uns farbige Kleider an.
Ich höre schon des Dorfs Getümmel,
Hier ist des Volkes wahrer Himmel,
Zufrieden jauchzet groß und klein:
Hier bin ich Mensch, hier darf ich's sein.

Easter Walk …

Just look and see the people fast
Scatter through gardens and the vale,
How then the river long and vast
Sees many a boat along there sail.
Through overload about to sink,
That last barge now away does slink.
And from the mountain's distant trail
Colourful clothes do us hail.
I hear already the village`s fray,
This is the people`s dearest day,
Contented cheer now grown and young:
»Here am I free, here do I belong.«

Der Rattenfänger

Ich bin der wohlbekannte Sänger,
Der vielgereis'te Rattenfänger,
Den diese altberühmte Stadt
Gewiss besonders nötig hat;
Und wären's Ratten noch so viele,
Und wären Wiesel mit im Spiele;
Von allen säubr' ich diesen Ort,
Sie müssen miteinander fort.

The Ratcatcher

I`m a singer who is famous,
As a ratcatcher I`m blameless,
Whom this long famed town
Certainly with pleasure found.
Were there rats in number many,
Or around there weasels any,
Of all would I clear this place,
Their chance would be run and race.

Der Rattenfänger …

Dann ist der gutgelaunte Sänger
Mitunter auch ein Kinderfänger,
Der selbst die wildesten bezwingt,
Wenn er die goldnen Märchen singt.
Und wären Knaben noch so trutzig,
Und wären Mädchen noch so stutzig,
In meine Saiten greif' ich ein,
Sie müssen alle hinterdrein.

Dann ist der vielgewandte Sänger
Gelegentlich ein Mädchenfänger;
In keinem Städtchen langt er an,
Wo er's nicht mancher angetan.
Und wären Mädchen noch so blöde,
Und wären Weiber noch so spröde:
Doch allen wird so liebebang
Bei Zaubersaiten und Gesang.

The Ratcatcher …

That blithe singer is quite clever
Luring children as a tempter,
Even wild ones can he beat,
With his fairy songs so sweet.
Were the lads yet still defiant,
Were the girls not really pliant,
Would my fiddle-string I find,
And they`ll follow close behind.

This singer also is quite shrewd,
At times he likes nice girls to choose,
No townlet that did see him come,
Had girls who could withstand his charm.
Were girls yet still that silly,
And the women shy and chilly:
All will surely soon be lovesick
Through the fiddle`s tune and magic.

Gefunden

Ich ging im Walde
So für mich hin,
Und nichts zu suchen,
Das war mein Sinn.

Im Schatten sah' ich
Ein Blümchen stehn,
Wie Sterne leuchtend,
Wie Äuglein schön.

Found

So lost in thought
I roamed the grove,
And wished for nought,
Not even a trove.

There hid I saw
A floret bloom,
Like stars aglow,
Like eyes so blue.

Gefunden …

Ich wollt' es brechen,
Da sagt' es fein:
»Soll ich zum Welken
Gebrochen sein?«

Ich grub's mit allen
Den Würzlein aus,
Zum Garten trug ich's
Am hübschen Haus.

Ich pflanzt' es wieder
Am stillen Ort;
Nun zweigt es immer
Und blüht so fort.

Found …

I wished to break it,
But it said no:
»Shall I now wilt
And die without hope?«

I lifted it all
With its roots so fine.
And did it haul
To the garden mine.

To plant it there
At a quiet site;
Now does it prosper
And blooms so bright.

Der Totentanz

Der Türmer, der schaut zu Mitten der Nacht
Hinab auf die Gräber in Lage;
Der Mond, der hat alles ins Helle gebracht;
Der Kirchhof, er liegt wie am Tage.
Da regt sich ein Grab und ein anderes dann:
Sie kommen hervor, ein Weib da, ein Mann,
In weißen und schleppenden Hemden.

Das reckt nun, es will sich ergetzen sogleich,
Die Knöchel zur Runde, zum Kranze,
So arm und so jung, und so alt und so reich;
Doch hindern die Schleppen am Tanze.
Und weil hier die Scham nun nicht weiter gebeut,
Sie schütteln sich alle, da liegen zerstreut
Die Hemdelein über den Hügeln.

The Dance Of The Dead

The warder, he looks in the middle of night
Down on the graves in a row;
The moon, she lets all look alight;
The churchyard does itself show.
There moves a grave and another one then:
They come out gently, a woman and a man,
In whitish and loose dragging shrouds.

That stretches and wishes to feast at once,
The bones already form a fast round,
So poor and so rich and so old and so young;
Yet the trails are a hindrance to their bound.
As chastity isn`t any more their care,
They shake themselves all and there and there,
The sheets shaken-off lie spread on the graves.

Der Totentanz …

Nun hebt sich der Schenkel, nun wackelt das Bein,
Gebärden da gibt es vertrackte;
Dann klippert's und klappert's mitunter hinein,
Als schlüg' man die Hölzlein zum Takte.
Das kommt nun dem Türmer so lächerlich vor;
Da raunt ihm der Schalk, der Versucher, ins Ohr:
»Geh! Hole dir einen der Laken.«

Getan wie gedacht! Und er flüchtet sich schnell
Nun hinter geheiligte Türen.
Der Mond, und noch immer er scheinet so hell
Zum Tanz, den sie schauderlich führen.
Doch endlich verlieret sich dieser und der,
Schleicht eins nach dem andern gekleidet einher,
Und, husch, ist es unter dem Rasen.

The Dance Of The Dead …

Now wobbles a leg, now rises a thigh,
Movements are there twisted,
It rattles and jangles a lot for a while,
It sounds like a beat by bones assisted.
The warder yet thought it not really dear;
There whispered a voice, the Tempter, in his ear:
»Go get yourself one of the shrouds!«

He acts as planned and does then hide
Behind those doors once sainted.
The moon, and she still shines that bright
On their dancing, that`s spookily strained.
Yet finally disappear singly the ghosts,
Sneak one by one about fully clothed,
And woosh are they back underground.

Der Totentanz …

Nur einer, der trippelt and stolpert zuletzt
Und tappet und grapst an den Grüften,
Doch hat kein Geselle so schwer ihn verletzt,
Er wittert das Tuch in den Lüften.
Er rüttelt die Turmtür, sie schlägt ihn zurück,
Geziert und gesegnet, dem Türmer zum Glück,
Sie blinkt von metallenen Kreuzen.

Das Hemd muss er haben, da rastet er nicht,
Da gilt auch kein langes Besinnen,
Den gotischen Zierrat ergreift nun der Wicht
Und klettert von Zinne zu Zinnen.
Nun ist's um den armen, den Türmer getan!
Es ruckt sich von Schnörkel zu Schnörkel hinan,
Langbeinigen Spinnen vergleichbar.

The Dance Of The Dead …

But one, who scampers and stumbles at last
And raps and gropes at the tomb,
Yet none of his fellows has hurt him that hard,
He senses the shroud in the gloom.
He shakes at the tower door, it pushes him back,
Ornate and blessed, to the warder`s luck,
Metallic crosses are flashing.

There is no doubt, the shroud he must get,
He acts at once and takes his chance,
The Gothic turret the midget does grab
And climbs now from arch to arch.
The warder`s fear for his life is now deep!
It creeps up the scrollwork with enormous speed,
It looks like a long-legged spider.

Der Totentanz ...

Der Türmer erbleichet, der Türmer erbebt,
Gern gäb' er ihn wieder, den Laken.
Da häkelt – jetzt hat er am längsten gelebt –
Den Zipfel ein eiserner Zacken.
Schon trübet der Mond sich verschwindenden Scheins,
Die Glocke, sie donnert ein mächtiges Eins,
Und unten zerschellt das Gerippe.

The Dance Of The Dead …

The warder turns pale, the warder is shaken,
Would like to hand back the scaring sheet.
There catches – he now feels his life sure taken -
The corner on a metal piece.
The light of the moon is almost now gone,
In darkness the bell, it thunders a one,
Down there the carcass smashes to pieces.

Regenbogen

Über den Hügeln einer anmutigen Landschaft

Grau und trüb und immer trüber
Kommt ein Wetter angezogen;
Blitz und Donner sind vorüber,
Euch erquickt ein Regenbogen.

Frohe Zeiten zu gewahren,
Wird der Erdkreis nimmer müde;
Schon seit vielen tausend Jahren
Spricht der Himmelsbogen: Friede!

Rainbow

Over the hills of a lovely countryside

Grey and dreary and still duller
Comes the weather causing row:
Thunder, lightning are now over,
And a rainbow cheers you all.

Merry times to safeguard well,
Will the globe sure never cease.
Many thousand years can tell,
The arch of heaven heralds peace!

Regenbogen …

Aus des Regens düstrer Trübe
Glänzt das Bild, das immer neue;
In den Tränen zarter Liebe
Spiegelt sich der Engel –Treue.

Wilde Stürme, Kriegeswogen
Rasten über Hain und Dach;
Ewig doch und allgemach
Stellt sich her der bunte Bogen.

Über Wiese, Hain und Dach
Stürzte Krieges Ungemach,
Wo nun Frühlingslüftchen fächelt
Und der Friedensbogen lächelt.

Rainbow …

After rainy days so rough,
Shines the sight and always new;
In the tears of tender love
Is reflected the angel – true.

Tempests rough and wars` uproar
Raced across our roof and grove.
Forever and throughout then though
Presents the world its motley flow.

Over meadow, roof and grove
Did war's dire horror rove,
Where spring's air now kindly fans
And the all-embracing peace now reigns.

Das Mädchen Spricht

Du siehst so ernst, Geliebter! Deinem Bilde
Von Marmor hier möcht' ich dich wohl vergleichen;
Wie dieses gibst du mir kein Lebenszeichen;
Mit dir verglichen zeigt der Stein sich milde.

Der Feind verbirgt sich hinter seinem Schilde,
Der Freund soll offen seine Stirn uns reichen.
Ich suche dich, du suchst mir zu entweichen;
Doch halte stand, wie dieses Kunstgebilde.

An wen von beiden soll ich nun mich wenden?
Sollt ich von beiden Kälte leiden müssen,
Da dieser tot und du lebendig heißest?

Kurz, um der Worte mehr nicht zu verschwenden,
So will ich diesen Stein so lange küssen,
Bis eifersüchtig du mich ihm entreißest.

The Girl Is Speaking

You look so grave, my lord! That image
Of marble made would I with you compare.
Like it you do not show me that you care.
Whereas the stone`s face looks at me less frigid.

The enemy does hide behind his shield,
The friend shall show his brow us openly.
I look for you, you try to run away from me,
Yet please do stay, like this so stony build.

To whom shall I of you two willingly now turn?
Must I from both of you now suffer icy feel,
Since that one`s dead and you're apparently alive?

In short, so not to waste another useless word,
I want to kiss that stone so long, it is a deal,
Until your jealousy will let your love then newly thrive.

Frühling Übers Jahr

Das Beet, schon lockert
Sich's in die Höh',
Da wanken Glöckchen
So weiß wie Schnee;
Safran entfaltet
Gewalt'ge Glut,
Smaragden keimt es
Und keimt wie Blut.

Primeln stolzieren
So naseweis,
Schalkhafte Veilchen,
Versteckt mit Fleiß;
Was auch noch alles
Da regt und webt,
Genug, der Frühling
Er wirkt und lebt.

Spring Again

The soil breaks up,
Begins to rise,
And little bells
Wave snow-like white,
Safran emits
Prodigious glow,
Emeralds sprout,
Do gorgeously grow.

Primroses strut
Along with pride,
Cheeky violets
Their blooms do hide;
Whatever stirs
And moves about,
Enough, it`s spring
That`s reigning now.

Frühling Übers Jahr ...

Doch was im Garten
Am reifsten blüht,
Das ist des Liebchens
Lieblich Gemüt.
Da glühen Blicke
Mir immerfort,
Erregend Liedchen,
Erheiternd Wort.

Ein immer offen,
Ein Blütenherz,
Im Ernste freundlich
Und rein im Scherz.
Wenn Ros' und Lilie
Der Sommer bringt,
Er doch vergebens
Mit Liebchen ringt.

Spring Again …

Yet what in the garden
Now blooms so good,
That is my darling`s
Delightful mood.
I feel her look
Blaze without cease,
Exciting her singing,
Her talking does please.

A heart always kind,
That reminds of a bloom,
When serious, friendly,
In jest doesn`t doom.
When rose and lily
The summer will bring,
Against its power
Her charm yet will win.

Um Mitternacht

Um Mitternacht ging ich, nicht eben gerne,
Klein, kleiner Knabe, jenen Kirchhof hin
Zu Vaters Haus, des Pfarrers; Stern am Sterne,
Sie leuchteten doch alle gar zu schön;
Um Mitternacht.

Wenn ich dann ferner in des Lebens Weite
Zur Liebsten musste, musste, weil sie zog,
Gestirn und Nordschein über mir im Streite,
Ich gehend, kommend Seligkeiten sog;
Um Mitternacht.

Bis dann zuletzt des vollen Mondes Helle
So klar und deutlich mir ins Finstere drang,
Auch der Gedanke willig, sinnig, schnelle
Sich ums Vergangne wie ums Künftige schlang;
Um Mitternacht.

At Midnight

At midnight I would go, but was not glad,
A little lad, across the churchyard there,
To fathers` manse, brightest star overhead
They shone, they all, up there so fair;
At midnight.

When I advanced in life`s large field
Then hurried, called, my love to kiss,
I saw the stars and Northern Lights compete,
My leaving, coming caused pure bliss;
At midnight.

Until the full moon´s brightness then at last,
My thinking`s darkness plainly did pervade
And so the mind now willing, musing, fast,
Things past and future did embrace;
At Midnight.

Du Hattest Längst Mir's Angetan

Du hattest längst mir's angetan,
Doch jetzt gewahr' ich neues Leben;
Ein süßer Mund blickt uns gar freundlich an,
Wenn er uns einen Kuss gegeben.

Tadelt man, dass wir uns lieben,
Dürfen wir uns nicht betrüben,
Tadel ist von keiner Kraft.
Andern Dingen mag das gelten,
Kein Missbilligen, kein Schelten
Macht die Liebe tadelhaft.

You Sure Had Won Long Since My Heart

You sure had won long since my heart,
Yet now a new life stirs my mind;
So sweet a mouth gives us a laugh,
When it is kissing us so kind.

Be blamed for loving one another,
Should never cause us any bother,
Reproof`s an act without much force.
In other moments may that help.
No chiding nor just disapproval
Can ever let love look yet coarse.

Dem Aufgehenden Vollmonde

Willst du mich sogleich verlassen?
Warst im Augenblick so nah!
Dich umfinstern Wolkenmassen,
Und nun bist du gar nicht da.

Doch du fühlst, wie ich betrübt bin,
Blickt dein Rand herauf als Stern!
Zeugest mir, dass ich geliebt bin,
Sei das Liebchen noch so fern.

So hinan denn! hell und heller,
Reiner Bahn, in voller Pracht!
Schlägt mein Herz auch schmerzlich schneller,
Überselig ist die Nacht.

To The Rising Moon

Will you leave me yet so soon?
Were so close to me right now!
Bulks of clouds surround all you,
Thus you are no more about.

But you feel how much I grieve,
Up there shows your rim as star!
Tells me my love thinks of me,
Even if she`s now so far.

So now rise! Grow bright and brighter,
Run your orbit in all splendour!
If my heart beats sorely faster,
Overjoyed is night`s great grandeur.

Anhang

Appendix

Nachwort

Goethes literarisches Wirken endete mit seinem Tod im Jahre 1832. Sein literarisches Schaffen beeinflusst bis heute unsere moderne Gesellschaft in Schulen, in Universitäten, in Theatern, im Internet und im Fernsehen. So kennen die meisten Menschen die Schlüsselfiguren in seinen Dramen wie Werther, Faust, Mephistopheles usw. Sie alle haben dazu beigetragen, unser moralisches und intellektuelles Verständnis der Welt zu formen. Seine Prosa ist, wenn man so will, allgegenwärtig.

Was ist mit seinem lyrischen Werk? Gibt es darin etwas, das unser Interesse weckt, das wir gerne lesen. Etwas, das unsere Phantasie anregt, das Gefühle anspricht, die unser eigenes Leben berühren? Um Antworten auf diese Fragen zu finden, haben wir dieses Projekt gestartet und einige seiner bekanntesten Gedichte und Balladen herausgegeben, in der Hoffnung, dass sie Reaktionen wie »Oh, ja! Ich erinnere mich an sie« oder »Es ist toll, sie wieder zu lesen« auslösen.

Und für diejenigen, die die englische Sprache mögen, haben wir eine Nachdichtung in englischer Sprache herausgebracht.

Annotations

Up to his death in the year 1832 Goethe continued focussing on his creative work. His literary remains have still a great impact on today`s thinking and especially on drama. His works are read, played and researched in schools, universities, theatres, the Internet or on Television. So most people know about the key characters in his dramas like Werther, Faust, Mephistopheles etc. , which have helped form our moral and intellectual understanding of the world. His prose work is, one might say, ever-present.

What about his lyrical work? Do we find there anything which may rouse our interest, we may love reading, that can stir our imagination, which addresses feelings that touch our own life? To find answers to these questions we have started this project of editing some of his best known poems and ballads hoping they may cause reactions like »Oh, yes! I remember them« or »It`s great to read them again«.

Those who like the English language can read Goethe`s poems in that language.

Albrecht Kienow, Anglist und Gymnasiallehrer an einem Wiesbadener Gymnasium, hat sich seit seiner Pensionierung die Freude an der englischen Sprache stets bewahrt. Über Theodor Storm (Stormliederbuch, 2022) hat er sich Goethe auf eine sprachliche Weise genähert und ihn genossen. Dabei heraus kam seine ganz eigene Nachdichtung in englischer Sprache. Als Herausgeber für Lyrik brauchte er mich nicht lange zu überzeugen, seine Dichtungen zu veröffentlichen.

Kronberg, 25.03.2025

Albrecht Kienow, an anglicist and former teacher at a grammar school has begun, after his retirement, to engage himself in adapting selected lyrical works of romantic poets using the English language. He started with the songbook of Theodor Storm, which is already available on the market. When he realized that he could do such translations successfully, he chose Goethe as the next poet and on careful deliberation he decided to discuss with me if it made sense to present also this new adaptation of Goethe`s poems to a larger public. In the end he and I thought that we should venture the step of going public with his adaptations.

Kronberg, 25.03.2025

Anmerkungen zur Quellenlage einzelner Gedichte:

Wechsel:
In der Hamburger Ausgabe nicht enthalten. Siehe hier: Quelle 3 im Literaturverzeichnis.

An Die Entfernte:
Anders als bei www.zeno.org ,die die Entstehung des Gedichts auf das Jahr 1788 datieren, sind auch wir eher der Meinung von Dr. Lehmann, dass mit »An die Entfernte« hier wohl Fredericke von Brion gemeint sei. Siehe hier: Quelle 3 im Literaturverzeichnis.

Regenbogen:
In der Hamburger Ausgabe nicht enthalten. Zu finden zum Beispiel in der Cotta'schen Ausgabe in 6 Bänden, Band 1, S. 450, Tübingen 1854. Siehe auch im Literaturverzeichnis.

Wir weisen darauf hin, dass wir das Gedicht Regenbogen, anders als im Internet, hier mit 5 Strophen veröffentlichen! Siehe hierzu Quelle 5 im Literaturverzeichnis.

Notes on the sources of individual poems:

Change:
The Hamburg Edition does not contain this poem.
Compare source 3 in the register.

To The Distant:
The Internet address www.zeno.org holds that the
publication of the poem dates from the year 1778, whereas
we, just like Dr. Lehmann, believe that the woman
addressed in the poem »To The Distant« was Fredericke
von Brion. Source 3 in the register.

Rainbow
This poem is not mentioned in the Hamburg Edition. We
found it in the Cotta Edition, volume 1, page 450,
published 1854 in Tübingen. Compare the register.

*We would like to point out that we publish 5 verses of the
poem »Rainbow« different from the 4 verses that can be found
in the Internet. Compare source 5 in the register.*

Unser Team ...

...Anni Vornberg, die den deutschen Text im Abgleich mit der Literatur Korrektur gelesen hat,

...Albrecht Kienow, der sich der großen Aufgabe einer Nachdichtung auf Englisch gewidmet hat,

...Anne Kunze, die die englischen Texte zusammen mit Herrn Kienow lektoriert hat.

...Peter Vornberg, der als Kronberger Künstler das Projekt ins Leben gerufen hat.

...Susanne Schmitt, die das Nachwort auf Rechtschreibfehler geprüft hat.

...Peter Schulte, Herausgeber

Our Team …

… Anni Vornberg, who made sure that the German texts correspond as to spelling and completeness of contents with the literary originals.

…Albrecht Kienow, who adapted a selected number of Goethe`s poems and ballads to the English language.

…Anne Kunze who helped by proofreading Mr. Kienow`s English texts.

…Peter Vornberg, a lyric and photo artist living in Kronberg, who has initiated the project of publishing a selection of Goethe`s lyrical work.

…Susanne Schmitt who has taken care of the correct spelling with the annotations

…Peter Schulte, Editor

Literaturverzeichnis / Quellenverzeichnis

Primär- und Sekundärquellen Bücher: Quellen Q1 bis Q5 (und Q6 als Referenzquelle für Abgleich der Satzzeichen mit Q1, Q3):

(1) Johann Wolfgang von Goethe, Hamburger Ausgabe in 14 Bänden, 16. Durchgesehene Auflage (Erich Trunz), dtv Verlag, München, 1996 (Copyrights C.H. Beck'sche Verlagsbuchhandlung, München)

(2) Johann Wolfgang von Goethe, Gedichte Ausgabe letzter Hand 1827, Berliner Ausgabe, 4. Auflage, bearbeitet und eingerichtet von Michael Holzinger, Henricus, Berlin, 2016

(3) Johann Wolfgang von Goethe, Goethes Liebe und Liebesgedichte, Dr. Lehmann, Johann August Otto Ludwig (Verfasser und Kommentator), Berlin: Allgemeine deutsche Verlags-Anstalt, 1852

(4) Johann Wolfgang Goethe, Goethes sämtliche Werke in sechs Bänden, Erster Band, Cotta'scher Verlag, Tübingen, 1854.

(5) Johann Wolfgang Goethe, Goethes sämtliche Werke in 45 Bänden, hier 38. Band; Propyläen-Ausgabe, Verlag: München, Georg Müller, 1909-1914, Erscheinungsdatum: 1909

(6) Johann Wolfgang von Goethe, Goethe Gedichte, Bd. 44 + 45, Deutscher Klassiker Verlag, Berlin 2010

Bibliography / List of References

We do not provide literary references to Goethe`s
works and publications in English.
Use the German references on the left-hand side or
consult sources in the Internet, where you might find
the information in English.

Literaturverzeichnis / Quellenverzeichnis ...

Primär- und Sekundärquellen für dieses Buch:

Internetquellen (Zugriff v. 01.02. – 01.09.2022):

(7) http://www.zeno.org/Literatur/M/Goethe,+Johann+Wolfgang/Gedichte

(8) https://www.projekt-gutenberg.org/goethe/gedichte/index.html

Weiterführende Literatur & Informationen über Johann Wolfgang Goethe und sein Gesamtwerk:

Das Romantikmuseum in Frankfurt am Main:
https://deutsches-romantik-museum.de/

Das Goethehaus in Frankfurt: Internetadresse siehe
Romantikmuseum

Das Goethe Nationalmuseum in Weimar:
https://www.klassik-stiftung.de/goethe-nationalmuseum/

Bibliography / List of References ...

Further reading & information about Johann Wolfgang von Goethe and his complete works:

The German Romanticism Museum in Frankfurt am Main:
https://deutsches-romantik-museum.de/en/

The Frankfurter Goethe House in Frankfurt am Main:
See Website above

The Goethe National Museum in Weimar:
https://www.klassik-stiftung.de/en/goethe-national-museum/

Literaturverzeichnis Gedichte	
Seite:	Daten:
10-12	Entstanden 1767/68, Erstdruck 1769, Q3
14	Entstanden Ende 1760, Erstdruck 1769, Q3
16	Entstanden Anfang 70er Jahre, Erstdruck 1789, Q3
18-22	Entstanden 1771, Erstdruck 1775, Q3
24-26	Entstanden 1771, Erstdruck 1789, Q3
28	Entstanden 1771, Q1
30-32	Entstehung 1771, Erstdruck 1775 (Frühe Fassung), Q1
34-36	Entstanden 1774/75, Erstdruck 1775, Q3
38-40	Entstanden, 1774,Erstdruck 1782, Q1, Q3
42	Entstanden, 1776,Erstdruck 1789, Q1
44	Entstanden 1776, Erstdruck 1789, Q1
46-50	Entstanden 1778, Erstdruck 1779, Q1
52-58	Entstanden 1780 – 1782, Erstdruck 1782, Q1
60	Entstanden 1780, Erstdruck 1815, Q1
62	Entstehung 1788, Erstdruck 1788, Q1
64-68	Entstanden 1789, Erstdruck 1789 (Spätere Fassung), Q1, alt. Q3

Bibliography Poems	
Page:	Data:
11-13	Year of origin 1767/68, Year of first printing 1769
15	Year of origin end of 60s, Year of first printing 1769
17	Year of origin 1867, Year of first printing 1868
19-23	Year of origin 1771, Year of first printing 1775
25-27	Year of origin 1771, Year of first printing 1789
29	Year of origin 1771
31-33	Year of origin 1771, Year of first printing 1775 (Early Version)
35-37	Year of origin 1774/75, Year of first printing 1775
39-41	Year of origin 1774, Year of first printing 1782
43	Year of origin 1776, Year of first printing 1789
45	Year of origin 1776, Year of first printing 1789
47-51	Year of origin 1778, Year of first printing 1779
53-59	Year of origin 1880–1782, Year of first printing 1782
61	Year of origin 1780, Year of first printing 1815
63	Year of origin 1788, Year of first printing 1788
65-69	Year of origin 1789 (Later Version), Year of first printing 1789

Literaturverzeichnis Gedichte ...	
Seite:	Daten:
72	Entstanden 1795, Q1
74-78	Entstanden 1797, Erstdruck 1797, Q1
80-94	Entstanden 1797, Erstdruck 1797, Q1
96-100	Entstanden 1801, Erstdruck 1803, Q1 alt. Q3
102-106	Entstehung 1801, Erstdruck 1808 in Faust I, Eine Tragödie, Q1
108-110	Entstanden 1802/03, Erstdruck 1803/04, Q4
112-114	Entstanden 1813, Erstdruck 1815, Q3
116-122	Entstanden 1813, Erstdruck 1815, Q1
124-126	Entstanden?, Erstdruck ?, Q5 alle 5 Strophen!
128	Entstanden 1815/27, Erstdruck ? Enthalten in Goethes Sonett-Zyklus, Q1
130-132	Entstanden 1816, Erstdruck 1820, Q1
134	Entstanden 1818, Erstdruck 1821, Q1
136	Entstanden August 1823, Erstdruck? Q1
138	Entstanden 25. Aug. 1828, Erstdruck? Q1 alt Q3

Bibliography Poems ...	
Page:	Data:
73	Year of origin 1795
75-79	Year of origin 1797, Year of first printing 1797
81-95	Year of origin 1797, Year of first printing 1797
97-101	Year of origin 1801, Year of first printing 1803
103-107	Year of origin 1801, Year of first printing 1808 in Faust I, A Tragedy,
109-111	Year of origin 1802, Year of first printing 1803/04
113-115	Year of origin 1813, Year of first printing 1815
117-123	Year of origin 1813, Year of first printing 1815
125-127	Year of origin ?, Year of first printing ?
129	Year of origin 1815/27, Year of first printing? Contained in Goethe's sonnet cycle
131-133	Year of origin 1816, Year of first printing 1820
135	Year of origin 1818, Year of first printing 1821
137	Year of origin 1823, Year of first printing ?
139	Year of origin 1828, Year of first printing 1864

Erstellung Buchblock: Peter Vornberg (Kronberg)
Grafik: iku4/ Shutterstock.com
Autor: Johann Wolfgang von Goethe
Nachdichtung: Albrecht Kienow (Schlangenbad)
Herausgeber:
Peter Schulte (Editor), Friedrichstraße 72, 61476 Kronberg in Taunus
E-Mail:peter.schulte_malerblick+goethe@mailbox.org
Auslieferung:
1. Auflage: März 2025
Verlag: BoD · Books on Demand GmbH, Überseering 33,
22297 Hamburg, bod@bod.de
Druck: Libri Plureos GmbH, Friedensallee 273, 22763 Hamburg
ISBN-Softcover: 978-3-7693-0141-0

Bibliografische Information der Deutschen Nationalbibliothek: Die
Deutsche Nationalbibliothek verzeichnet diese Publikation in der
Deutschen Nationalbibliografie; detaillierte bibliografische Daten sind
im Internet über dnb.dnb.de abrufbar.

©/ Copyright: 2025 Peter Schulte (Editor)

Compilation of the texts: Peter Vornberg (Kronberg)
Graphic: iku4/ Shutterstock.com
Author: Johann Wolfgang von Goethe
Adaptation in English: Albrecht Kienow (Schlangenbad)
Editor:
Peter Schulte, Friedrichstraße 72, 61476 Kronberg/Taunus
E-Mail: peter.schulte_malerblick+goethe@mailbox.org
Publication:
First edition: March 2025
Production and Publisher: BoD · Books on Demand GmbH,
Überseering 33, 22297 Hamburg, bod@bod.de
Print: Libri Plureos GmbH, Friedensallee 273, 22763 Hamburg
ISBN-Softcover: 978-3-7693-0141-0

Bibliographic Information of the German National Library: The German National Library lists this publication in the German National Bibliography; detailed bibliographic data is available on the Internet at dnb.dnb.de.